springtime

Story by Marie Sumalee
Illustrated by Lori Berlot

I see a beautiful rainbow
while riding on my bike.

I see many butterflies,
kites and dragonflies
flying in the sky.

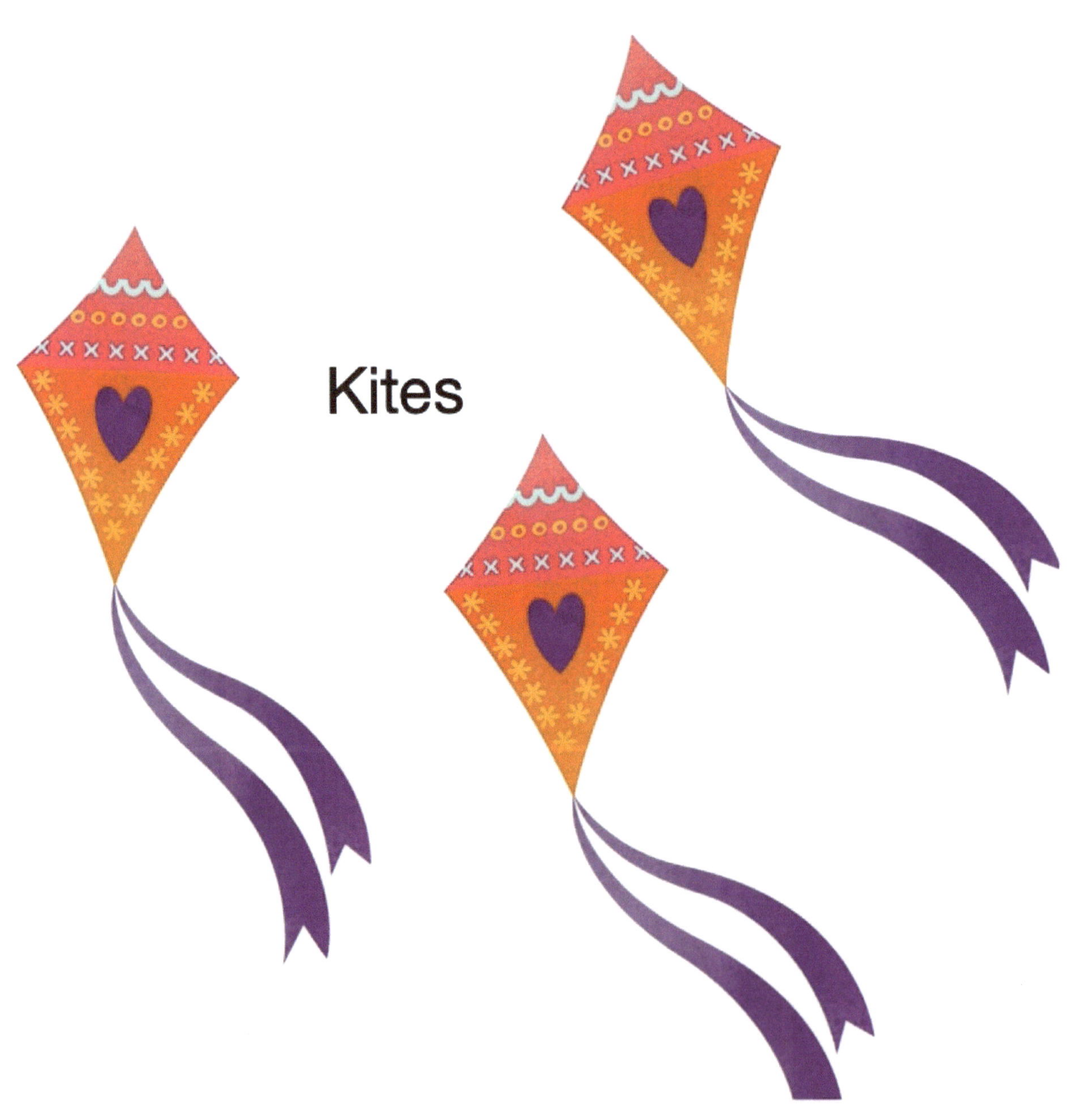

Kites

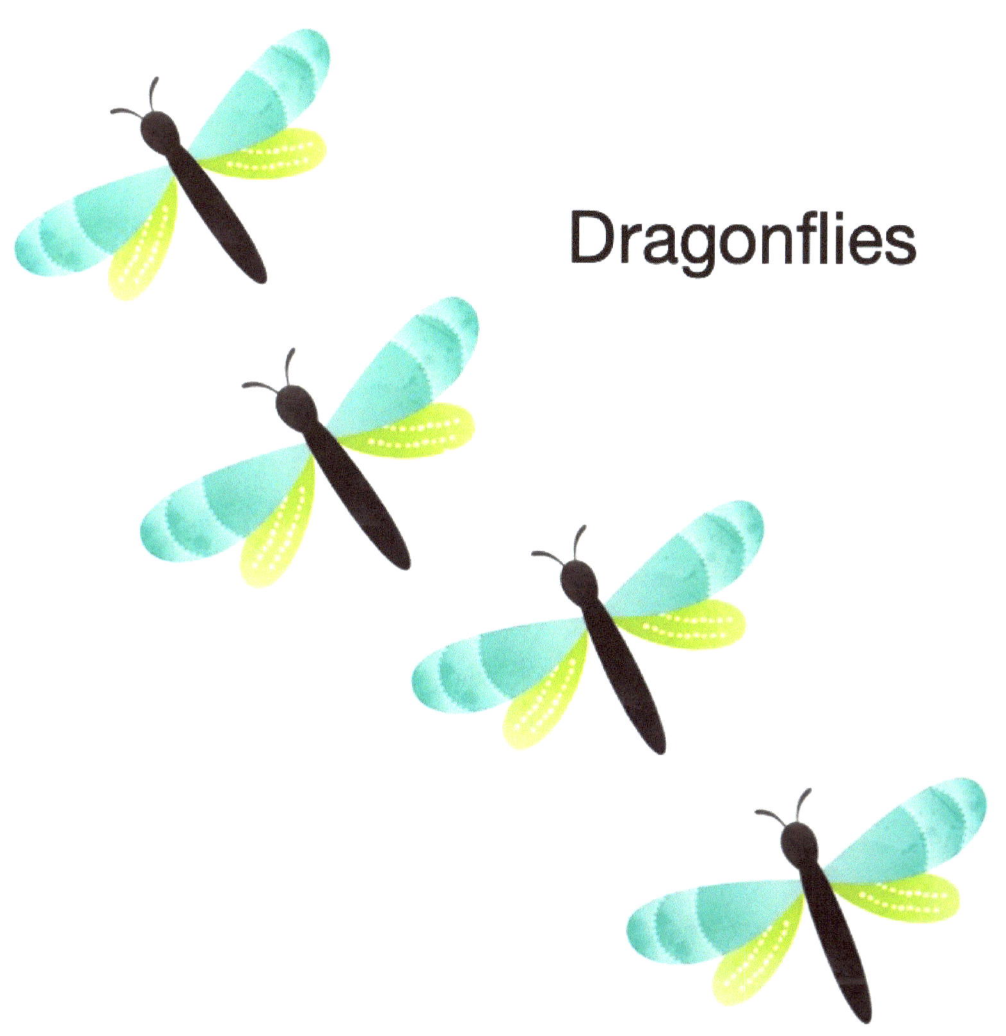

Dragonflies

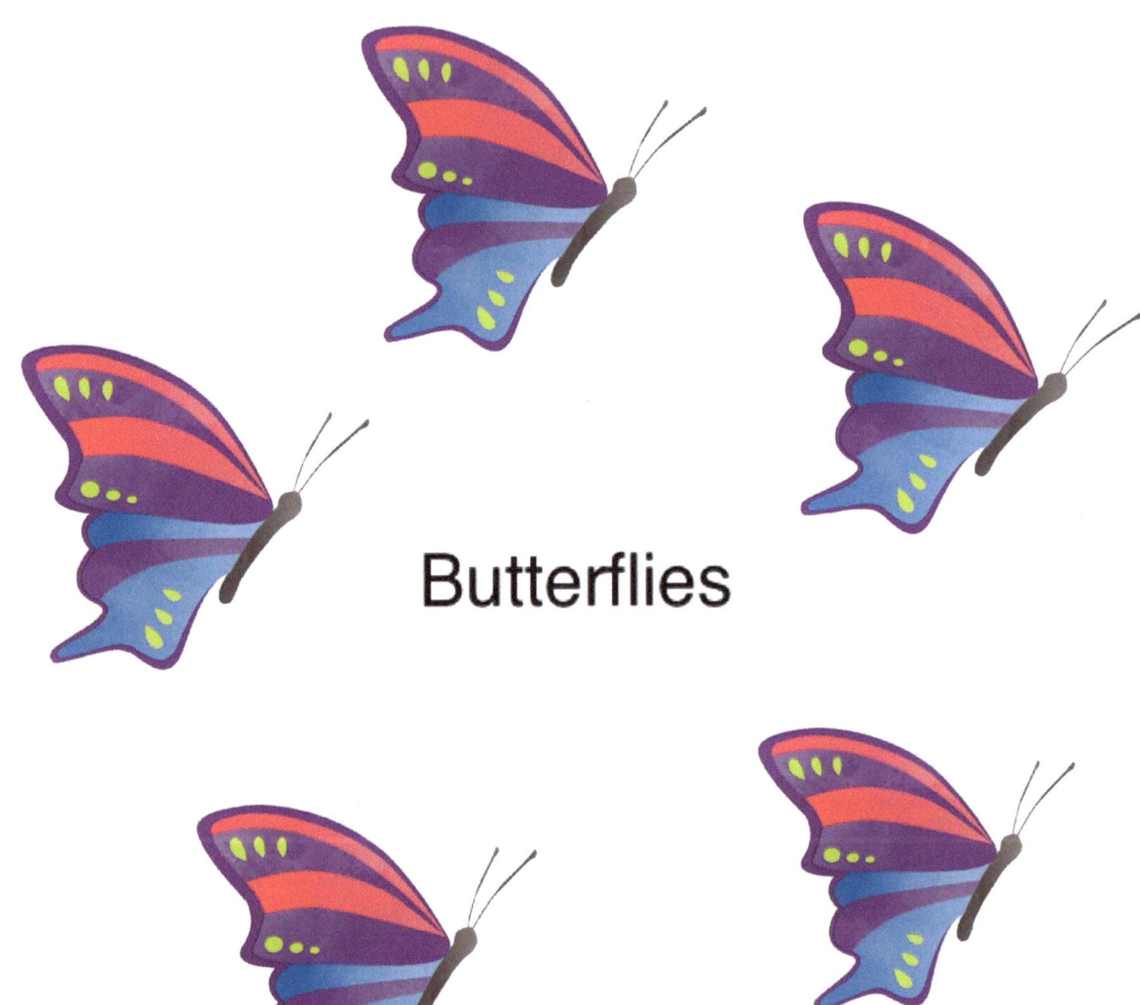

Butterflies

I put on my rubber
boots so my feet
won't get wet.

I water the flowers
with a watering can.

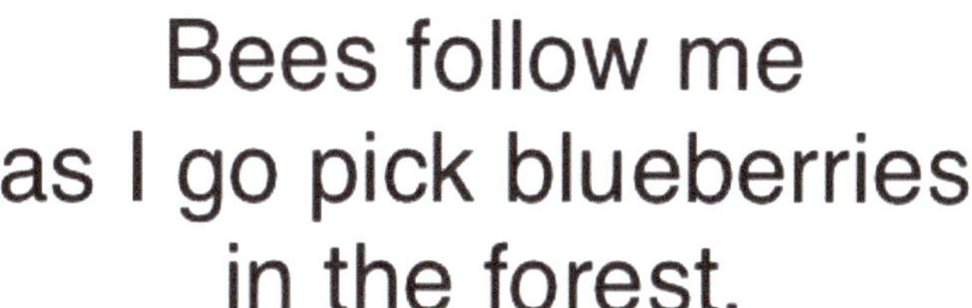

Bees follow me
as I go pick blueberries
in the forest.

In the forest,
I see birds and
rabbits.

The foxes are out
to play.

I see many colourful flowers.

Daisies
Green
leaves

I see blue leaves.

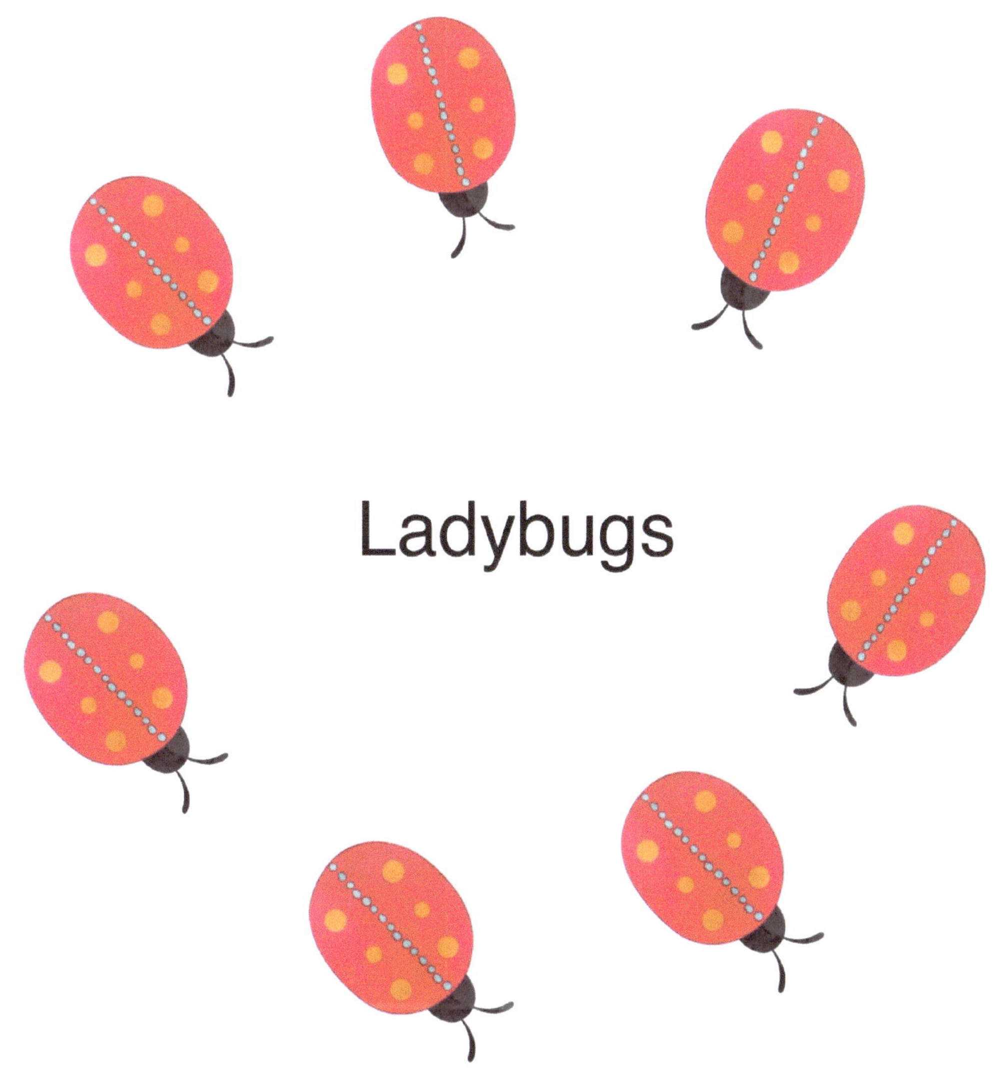

Ladybugs

I see many trees and plants of different colours.

Watering can

Rainbow

Fox

Green branch

Branch

Rubber boots

Pansies

Yellow Daisy

Blue leaves
Dragonfly
Banner
Kite

Blueberries

Butterfly

Ladybug

Gerbera Daisy

Cloud

Blue bird

Flower planter

Bicycle
Flowerpot
Bee
Rabbit

Happy Spring !

The End